SILVER PALATE
DESSERTS

SILVER PALATE
DESSERTS

Recipes from the Classic American Cookbooks

JULEE ROSSO AND SHEILA LUKINS
WITH MICHAEL McLAUGHLIN AND SARAH LEAH CHASE

Running Press
PHILADELPHIA • LONDON

CONTENTS

INTRODUCTION

". . . food has long been our passion. And we are fortunate to be involved professionally with what we call the miracle of food, at the outset of what is certain to be one of the most exhilarating culinary eras that America has ever enjoyed."

So wrote Sheila Lukins and Julee Rosso more than ten years ago, as they prepared to publish their *Silver Palate Cookbook*, a work that has changed the way Americans look at food, cooking, and entertaining.

Rosso and Lukins created their book in response to a rapidly growing appreciation for fine foods in America. Whether inspired by the authors' travels, adapted from favorites shared with them by friends and colleagues, or created as contemporary versions of traditional dishes, the Silver Palate recipes are the embodiment of a new and uniquely American cooking style.

The Silver Palate Cookbook and its sequels, *The Silver Palate Good Times Cookbook* and *The New Basics Cookbook*, quickly spread that style from coast to coast, to millions of picnics, brunches, and dinners. Together, the three books have sold more than four million copies.

Silver Palate dessert recipes, in particular, have brought new flavors and textures—some delicate and some decadently rich—to cookies and cakes, tarts and tortes, ices and mousses. Lightly topped off with crème fraîche or oozing with chocolate fudge sauce, the desserts selected for this book are favorites from *The Silver Palate Cookbook* and

The Silver Palate Good Times Cookbook. With illustrations by Sheila Lukins, here are recipes for Chocolate Hazelnut Cake, Carrot Cake, Blackberry Mousse, Kumquat Citrus Tarts, Toffee Bars, and more than two dozen other innovative confections.

Warm and accessible, *Silver Palate Desserts* presents a delectable sampling from the cookbooks that have set the standard for American cuisine.

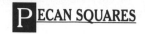PECAN SQUARES

These are like tiny pecan pies—chewy, gooey and thick with pecans. Try them slightly warmed as an accompaniment to good ice cream.

Crust:

²/₃ cup confectioners' sugar

2 cups unbleached all-purpose flour

½ pound (2 sticks) sweet butter, softened

1. Preheat oven to 350°F. Grease a 9 x 12 inch baking pan.
2. Sift sugar and flour together. Cut in butter, using two knives or a pastry blender, until fine crumbs form. Pat crust into the prepared baking pan. Bake for 20 minutes; remove from oven.

Topping:

⅔ cup (approximately 11 tablespoons) melted sweet butter

½ cup honey

3 tablespoons heavy cream

½ cup brown sugar

3½ cups shelled pecans, coarsely chopped

1. Mix melted butter, honey, cream, and brown sugar together. Stir in pecans, coating them thoroughly. Spread over crust.

2. Return to oven and bake for 25 minutes more. Cool completely before cutting into squares.

36 squares

TOFFEE BARS

Light, crisp, and chocolaty.

½ pound (2 sticks) sweet butter

1 cup light brown sugar

1 egg yolk

2 cups unbleached all-purpose flour

1 teaspoon vanilla extract

12 ounces
semisweet
chocolate chips

1 cup shelled
walnuts or pecans,
coarsely chopped

TOFFEE BARS

1. Preheat oven to 350°F. Grease a 9 x 12 inch baking pan.

2. Cream butter and sugar. Add egg yolk; beat well.

3. Sift in flour, mixing well, then stir in vanilla. Spread batter in the prepared pan. Bake for 25 minutes.

4. Cover cake layer with chocolate chips and return to oven for 3 to 4 minutes.

5. Remove pan from oven and spread melted chocolate evenly. Sprinkle with nuts. Cool completely in pan before cutting.

About 30 bars

BUTTERBALLS

While there are many versions of this cookie, this one has long been a Rosso Christmas tradition and is the best we know.

**8 tablespoons (1 stick)
sweet butter, softened**

3 tablespoons honey

1 cup unbleached all-purpose flour

1/2 teaspoon salt

1 tablespoon vanilla extract

**1 cup shelled pecans,
chopped moderately fine**

3/4 cup confectioners' sugar

BUTTERBALLS

1. Preheat oven to 300°F. Grease one or two cookie sheets.

2. Cream butter. Beat in honey; gradually mix in flour and salt, then vanilla. Add pecans. Wrap dough in plastic wrap and chill for 1 hour.

3. Form balls by hand, the size of quarters. Place 2 inches apart on the prepared cookie sheets. Bake for 35 to 40 minutes.

4. Remove from oven; as soon as cool enough to touch, roll in confectioners' sugar. Allow to cool and roll again in sugar.

About 36 cookies

SHORTBREAD HEARTS

Another Silver Palate favorite, good year-round, but essential on Valentine's Day.

¾ pound (3 sticks) sweet butter, softened

1 cup confectioners' sugar

3 cups unbleached all-purpose flour, sifted

½ teaspoon salt

½ teaspoon vanilla extract

¼ cup granulated sugar

SHORTBREAD HEARTS

1. Cream butter and confectioners' sugar together until light.

2. Sift flour and salt together and add to creamed mixture. Add vanilla and blend thoroughly.

3. Gather dough into a ball, wrap in wax paper, and chill for 4 to 6 hours.

4. Roll out chilled dough to $5/8$-inch thickness. Using a 3-inch-long heart-shaped cookie cutter, cut out cookies. Sprinkle tops with granulated sugar. Place cut-out cookies on ungreased cookie sheets and refrigerate for 45 minutes before baking.

5. Preheat oven to 325°F.

6. Bake for 20 minutes, or until just starting to color lightly; cookies should not brown at all. Cool on a rack.

20 cookies

BROWNIES

Traditional American brownies—what could be better?

½ pound (2 sticks) sweet butter

4 ounces unsweetened chocolate

4 eggs

2 cups granulated sugar

½ cup unbleached all-purpose flour

1 teaspoon vanilla extract

⅔ cup shelled walnuts, coarsely chopped

1. Preheat oven to 350°F. Grease and flour a 9 x 12 inch baking pan.

2. Melt butter and chocolate in the top part of a double boiler over boiling water. When melted, set aside to cool to room temperature.

3. Meanwhile, beat eggs and sugar until thick and lemon-colored; add vanilla. Fold chocolate mixture into eggs and sugar. Mix thoroughly.

4. Sift flour and fold gently into batter, mixing just until blended. Fold in walnuts.

5. Pour into the prepared pan. Bake for 25 minutes, or until center is just set. Do not overbake.

6. Allow brownies to cool in pan for 30 minutes before cutting into bars.

28 large brownies

ROCKY MOUNTAIN-CHIP COOKIES

We love the way chocolate dresses up these chewy cookies. Be sure you don't overbake them because they do harden as they cool.

½ cup (1 stick) margarine, room temperature

½ cup (1 stick) unsalted butter, room temperature

1 cup packed dark brown sugar

1 cup granulated sugar

2 eggs, lightly beaten

2 tablespoons milk

2 teaspoons vanilla extract

2 cups sifted unbleached all-purpose flour

ROCKY MOUNTAIN-CHIP COOKIES

1 teaspoon baking powder
1 teaspoon baking soda
1 teaspoon salt
2 cups quick-cooking oats
12 ounces semisweet chocolate chips
1 cup coarsely chopped walnuts

1. Cream the margarine, butter, and both sugars in a large mixer bowl until light and fluffy. Add the eggs, milk, and vanilla and beat until blended.

2. Sift the flour, baking powder, baking soda, and salt together and add to the butter mixture. Stir just until blended. Stir in the oats. Fold in the chocolate and walnuts.

3. Refrigerate the dough covered for at least 1 hour.

4. Preheat oven to 350°F. Grease cookie sheets.

5. Shape the dough into balls, using a rounded teaspoon for small cookies or a scant tablespoon for large. Flatten slightly into rounded disks. Place 2 inches apart on the prepared baking sheets. Bake until the edges are slightly browned but the cookies are still white, 8 to 10 minutes.

6. Remove from the oven and let cool on the sheets for 5 minutes. Remove to wire racks to cool completely.

100 small or 50 large cookies

MOLASSES COOKIES

These soft, chewy, spicy cookies are one of the store's most popular. Don't expect them to be crisp; they are not ginger-snaps. They stay moist, in an airtight tin, for at least a week.

12 tablespoons (1½ sticks) sweet butter

1 cup granulated sugar

¼ cup molasses

1 egg

1¾ cups unbleached all-purpose flour

½ teaspoon ground cloves

½ teaspoon ground ginger

1 teaspoon ground cinnamon

½ teaspoon salt

½ teaspoon baking soda

1. Preheat oven to 350°F.

2. Melt butter, add sugar and molasses, and mix thoroughly. Lightly beat egg and add to butter mixture; blend well.

3. Sift flour with spices, salt, and baking soda, and add to first mixture; mix. Batter will be wet.

4. Lay a sheet of foil on a cookie sheet. Drop tablespoons of cookie batter on foil, leaving 3 inches between the cookies. These will spread during the baking.

5. Bake until cookies start to darken, 8 to 10

minutes. Remove from oven while still soft.

Let cool on foil.

24 very large flat cookies

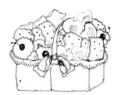

CHOCOLATE TRUFFLES

The most direct chocolate experience we know. Offer these confections to guests with coffee, or give them at holiday time.

1/4 cup heavy cream

2 tablespoons Grand Marnier

6 ounces German's sweet chocolate, broken up

4 tablespoons sweet butter, softened

powdered unsweetened cocoa

CHOCOLATE TRUFFLES

1. Boil cream in a small heavy pan until reduced to 2 tablespoons. Remove from heat, stir in Grand Marnier and chocolate, and return to low heat; stir until chocolate melts.

2. Whisk in softened butter. When mixture is smooth, pour into a shallow bowl and refrigerate until firm, about 40 minutes.

3. Scoop chocolate up with a teaspoon and shape into rough 1-inch balls. Roll the truffle balls in the unsweetened cocoa.

4. Store truffles, covered, in the refrigerator. Let truffles stand at room temperature for 30 minutes before serving.

24 truffles

Variations:

Substitute dark rum, Cognac, or another liqueur for the Grand Marnier. Try Kahlúa, Framboise, Crème de Menthe, or Amaretto.

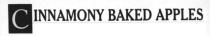

CINNAMONY BAKED APPLES

2 cups water

2¼ cups brown sugar

1½ tablespoons ground cinnamon

1½ tablespoons fresh lemon juice

6 medium-large tart baking apples,
   washed (do not peel)

¾ cup raisins

½ cup shelled pecans, chopped

1 tablespoon grated lemon zest

3 tablespoons Calvados
   or applejack

3 tablespoons sweet butter

1. Preheat oven to 375°F.

2. Mix water, 3/4 cup of the brown sugar, 1/2 tablespoon of the cinnamon and the lemon juice in a saucepan. Bring to a boil and cook for 3 minutes. Remove syrup from heat and reserve.

3. Remove the apple cores, but do not cut all the way through the bottoms.

4. In a bowl, mix remaining 1 1/2 cups brown sugar, the raisins, pecans, lemon zest, and remaining 1 tablespoon cinnamon. Fill each apple to within 1/4 inch of the top.

CINNAMONY BAKED APPLES

   Pour 1 teaspoon of applejack over the
   filling in each apple and top with
   1/2 tablespoon butter.

5. Transfer apples to a baking dish 9 x 13
   inches and pour syrup over apples. Pour
   remaining tablespoon of the applejack into
   the syrup.

6. Bake apples for 40 minutes, or until tender,
   basting them occasionally with syrup
   in pan.

7. When apples are done, transfer them with
   a slotted spoon to a serving dish. Pour
   syrup from pan into a small saucepan,
   bring to a boil, and cook until slightly

reduced, about 5 minutes. Cool slightly, pour a tablespoon of syrup over each apple and serve remaining syrup on the side.

6 portions

SOUR-CREAM APPLE PIE

A little slice goes a long way.

Crust:

2½ cups unbleached all-purpose flour

5 tablespoons granulated sugar

¾ teaspoon salt

¾ teaspoon ground cinnamon

6 tablespoons sweet butter, chilled

6 tablespoons shortening, chilled

4 to 6 tablespoons apple cider or juice, chilled

1. Sift flour, sugar, salt, and cinnamon into a bowl. Cut in butter and shortening with a fork or pastry cutter until mixture resembles rolled oats.
2. Moisten with just enough cider, tossing ingredients lightly with a fork, to permit the dough to be formed into a ball. Wrap and refrigerate for 2 hours.
3. Cut off one third of the dough and return it to the refrigerator. Roll out the other two thirds between 2 sheets of wax paper. Line a greased 9-inch pie pan with the dough. Trim overhang and crimp decoratively.
4. Preheat oven to 350°F.

Filling:

- **5 to 7 tart apples**
- **2/3 cup dairy sour cream**
- **1/3 cup granulated sugar**
- **1 egg, lightly beaten**
- **1/4 teaspoon salt**
- **1 teaspoon vanilla extract**
- **3 tablespoons unbleached all-purpose flour**

1. Peel, core and thinly slice apples; drop slices into a mixing bowl.

2. Whisk together sour cream, sugar, egg, salt, vanilla, and flour in a small bowl.

Pour mixture over apples and toss well
to coat. Spoon apples into pastry-lined
pie pan.

Topping:

3 tablespoons brown sugar

3 tablespoons granulated sugar

1 teaspoon ground cinnamon

1 cup shelled walnuts, chopped

1. Mix sugars, cinnamon, and walnuts
   together and sprinkle evenly over apple
   filling.
2. Roll out remaining pastry between sheets of
   wax paper to form a 10-inch circle.
   Cut into 1/2-inch strips, and arrange these

lattice-fashion over apples; trim ends of strips and crimp edge of crust decoratively.

3. Set pie on the middle rack of the oven and bake for 55 to 65 minutes. If crust browns too quickly, cover loosely with foil. Pie is done when juices are bubbling and apples are tender.

4. Serve warm or cool, topped, if you like, with whipped cream or vanilla ice cream.

6 portions

P EACH COBBLER

A dessert that brings memories of summer.

**4 cups peeled and sliced
ripe peaches**

**²/₃ cup plus 3 tablespoons
granulated sugar**

1 teaspoon grated lemon zest

1 tablespoon fresh lemon juice

¹/₄ teaspoon almond extract

1¹/₂ cups unbleached all-purpose flour

1 tablespoon baking powder

¹/₂ teaspoon salt

¹/₃ cup vegetable shortening

1 egg, lightly beaten

PEACH COBBLER

½ cup milk

1 cup heavy cream, chilled

3 to 4 tablespoons peach brandy or
    peach cordial

1. Preheat oven to 400°F. Butter a 2-quart baking dish.

2. Arrange peaches in baking dish. Sprinkle with 2/3 cup sugar, the lemon zest and juice, and almond extract.

3. Bake for 20 minutes.

4. While peaches are baking, sift flour, 1 tablespoon of the remaining sugar, the baking powder, and salt together into a bowl. Cut in shortening until mixture resembles cornmeal. Combine beaten egg and milk and mix into dry ingredients until just combined.

5. Remove peaches from oven and quickly drop dough by large spoonfuls over

surface. Sprinkle with remaining 2
tablespoons sugar. Return to the oven for
15 to 20 minutes, until top is firm and
golden brown.

6. Whip cream to soft peaks. Flavor with
peach brandy to taste.

7. Serve cobbler warm,
accompanied by
whipped cream.

4 to 6 portions

STRAWBERRY SHORTCAKE

One of our mothers long ago showed her spirit by announcing a dinner of only strawberry shortcake. Though we promised to keep it secret, we were typical elementary school students and couldn't wait for "Show and Tell" the next day. The memory of that dinner made the family laugh together for years.

STRAWBERRY SHORTCAKE

2 cups unbleached all-purpose flour

2 tablespoons granulated sugar

¾ teaspoon salt

1 tablespoon baking powder

4 tablespoons sweet butter, chilled

½ cup light cream

sweet butter, softened, for topping

6 cups strawberries, sliced and sugared to taste

1½ cups heavy cream, chilled

12 perfect strawberries (garnish)

1. Preheat oven to 450°F.

2. Sift flour, sugar, salt, and baking powder together into a mixing bowl.

3. Cut in the 4 tablespoons butter until mixture resembles oats. Pour in cream and mix gently until just blended.

4. Roll dough out on a floured work surface to a thickness of 5/8 inch. Cut into 3-inch circles with a cookie cutter. Gather scraps, roll again and cut more rounds; you should have 6 rounds.

5. Bake shortcakes on a greased baking sheet for about 10 minutes, or until puffed and lightly browned.

6. Cool the biscuits slightly, split them, and

spread softened butter lightly over the cut surfaces. Set the bottoms on dessert plates; spoon on sliced strawberries, and crown with the tops of the biscuits. Whip chilled cream, and spoon a dollop onto each shortcake, then garnish with a single perfect strawberry. Serve immediately.

6 shortcakes

Note:
To make drop biscuits, use an additional 1/4 cup cream and drop the dough by large spoonfuls onto the baking sheet. Bake as directed.

KUMQUAT CITRUS TARTS

A glistening kumquat half nestles on top of a rich citrus filling to make these miniature tarts pastry-shop perfect.

Pastry:

- **1½ cups unbleached all-purpose flour**
- **⅓ cup confectioners' sugar**
- **9 tablespoons unsalted butter, cold, cut into small pieces**
- **1 egg**
- **1 to 2 tablespoons ice water**

KUMQUAT CITRUS TARTS

Filling:

1 egg

1/3 cup granulated sugar

1 teaspoon finely grated
   orange zest

1 teaspoon finely grated lemon zest

2 tablespoons fresh lemon juice

2 tablespoons fresh orange juice

2 tablespoons heavy or
   whipping cream

Topping:

24 kumquats

1/3 cup Cointreau or other
   orange liqueur

Glaze:

⅓ cup apricot jam

2 tablespoons Cointreau or other orange liqueur

1. To make the pastry, process the flour, confectioners' sugar, and butter in a food processor fitted with a steel blade until the mixture resembles coarse meal. Add the egg. With the machine running, add enough of the water for the dough to gather into a ball. Do not overprocess. Wrap the dough in plastic wrap and refrigerate 2 hours.

2. Preheat oven to 400°F.

3. Divide the dough in half and roll out 1 half very thinly on a lightly floured surface. (Freeze the other half for another use.) Line sixteen 1-inch tart pans or small muffin cups with the dough. Trim the edges. Line each shell with waxed or parchment paper and weight with dried beans or pie weights. Bake on a baking sheet for 10 minutes. Remove the weights and let cool.

4. Reduce heat to 375°F.

5. To make the filling, process the egg, sugar, and orange and lemon zests in the food processor for 1 minute. Add the lemon and orange juices and the cream and process 30 seconds more.

6. Remove the paper from the shells and spoon 1 tablespoon of the citrus filling into each shell. Bake until the filling is set and lightly browned, about 15 minutes. Let cool to room temperature.

7. To make the topping, cut 8 of the kumquats in half and seed. Cut the remaining kumquats crosswise into thin slices and seed. Heat all the kumquats and the 1/3 cup Cointreau in a small enameled saucepan over medium heat to boiling. Cook, stirring constantly, until most of the liqueur has evaporated to form a syrupy coating over the kumquats.
Remove from heat.

KUMQUAT CITRUS TARTS

8. Remove the tarts from the pans. Make a circle of overlapping kumquat slices on top of each tart and place 1 kumquat half in the center.

9. To make the glaze, heat the apricot jam and 2 tablespoons Cointreau in a small saucepan until melted and smooth. Spoon the glaze over each tart.

Sixteen 1-inch tarts

ARVEST TART

1 cup pitted prunes

1 cup dried apricots

1 cup chopped peeled apples

½ cup golden raisins

⅓ cup granulated sugar

½ cup shelled walnut halves

¼ cup melted sweet butter

⅔ cup Grand Marnier

double recipe of Sweet Buttery
   Tart Crust (recipe follows)

1 egg, beaten

HARVEST TART

1. Preheat oven to 350°F.

2. Combine prunes, apricots, apples, and raisins in a heavy saucepan. Add water just to cover, set over moderate heat, and simmer until fruit is tender, about 20 minutes. Drain fruit thoroughly and chop.

3. Return fruit to saucepan, add sugar, walnuts, melted butter, and Grand Marnier, and simmer for 5 minutes, stirring occasionally. Cool to room temperature.

4. Roll out half of the pastry dough on a lightly floured board and use it to line a 9-inch pie pan. Spoon filling into pastry-lined pan, mounding it slightly. Trim excess

crust, leaving about 1 inch all around.

5. Roll out remaining dough to a 10½-inch round and cut into ½-inch strips. Arrange strips lattice-fashion over the filling, trim ends, and turn up the edge of the bottom crust over the ends of the strips; crimp decoratively. Brush lattice top lightly with beaten egg.

6. Bake tart for 30 to 35 minutes, or until top is golden brown and filling is bubbling. Serve warm or cool.

1 tart, 6 to 8 portions

S WEET BUTTERY TART CRUST

1²/₃ cups unbleached all-purpose
   flour

¹/₄ cup very fine granulated sugar

¹/₂ teaspoon salt

10 tablespoons (1¹/₄ sticks) sweet
   butter, chilled

2 egg yolks

1 teaspoon
   vanilla
   extract

2 teaspoons
   cold water

1. Sift flour, sugar, and salt into a mixing bowl. Cut chilled butter into pieces into the bowl. Using your fingertips, rapidly rub the butter and dry ingredients together until the mixture resembles coarse meal. Be careful to use only your fingertips as your palms will warm the dough.

2. Stir egg yolks, vanilla, and water together and add to the flour-butter mixture and blend in, using a fork. Shape dough into a ball. This should not take more than 30 to 45 seconds.

3. Place the ball of dough on a pastry board. With the heel of your hand, smear about 1/4 cup of dough away from you into a

6- to 8-inch smear; repeat until all dough has been dealt with. Scrape dough together; re-form into a ball, wrap in wax paper, and chill for 2 to 3 hours.

4. Roll out dough between 2 sheets of wax paper, or use a floured pastry cloth and floured stockinette on your rolling pin, into a round large enough to line your pan. Work quickly, as the dough can become sticky.

5. Line either an 8- or 9-inch false-bottom tart pan with the dough, fitting it loosely into pan and pressing to fit sides. Trim edges ¾ inch outside top of pan, and fold this

edge over to inside, and press into place with fingers. Chill.

6. Preheat oven to 425°F.

7. Line dough in the tart pan with a piece of aluminum foil or wax paper and weight with rice or beans. Bake for 8 minutes. Remove foil and beans. Prick the bottom of the dough with a fork in several places. For a partially baked shell, return to oven for 3 to 4 minutes longer. For a fully baked shell, return for 8 to 10 minutes longer, or until edges are a light brown.

One 8-inch to 9-inch tart shell

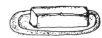

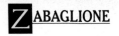

ZABAGLIONE

This dessert is wonderfully versatile, since it can be served hot or cold, is good by itself, and is even better as a topping for a combination of berries. We like equal parts of blueberries, raspberries, and strawberries.

8 egg yolks
3/4 cup granulated sugar
1/3 cup Marsala wine

1. Mix ingredients together in the top part of a double boiler and cook over rapidly boiling water, whisking constantly until mixture doubles in bulk and thickens.

2. Remove from heat and whisk for another minute.

3. Pour mixture warm over fresh berries, serve it in a tall glass by itself, or chill it and serve as a sauce for berries.

6 portions

Buy Fir-
Milk
ream
Salmon

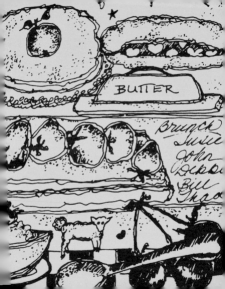

BUTTER

Brunch
Susie
John
Rebecca
Bill
Shaa

RHUBARB SORBET

A light pink, intensely flavored sorbet.

3 cups sliced fresh rhubarb

1 cup plus 2 tablespoons sugar

1½ cups water

3 tablespoons Cointreau

2 tablespoons framboise or
cassis liqueur

1 tablespoon fresh lemon juice

3 tablespoons heavy or
whipping cream

1. Place the rhubarb in a medium-size saucepan. Sprinkle with the sugar, and add $1/2$ cup of the water, the Cointreau, and framboise. Simmer until the rhubarb is tender and almost puréed, 15 to 20 minutes.

2. Process the fruit with its syrup, the lemon juice, and cream in a food processor fitted with a steel blade until smooth. Taste for sweetness and adjust with more lemon juice or sugar if necessary. Remove from the food processor and stir in the remaining 1 cup water.

3. Freeze in an ice cream maker, following manufacturer's instructions.

1 quart

CHOCOLATE FUDGE SAUCE

This is a deep, dark, fudgy sauce that hardens on ice cream to a thick, delicious glaze.

4 ounces unsweetened chocolate

3 tablespoons sweet butter

²/₃ cup water

1²/₃ cups granulated sugar

6 tablespoons corn syrup

1 tablespoon rum

1. Melt chocolate and butter very slowly in a heavy saucepan. Meanwhile, heat the water to boiling. When chocolate and butter have melted, add water and stir well.

2. Add the sugar and corn syrup and mix until smooth. Turn the heat up and stir until mixture starts to boil; adjust the heat so that sauce is just maintained at the boiling point. Allow the sauce to boil, without stirring, for 9 minutes.

3. Remove sauce from heat and cool for 15 minutes. Stir in the rum. Serve sauce warm over ice cream or pastries.

2½ cups

R ASPBERRY-SAUTERNES DESSERT SOUP

On the hottest day of the hottest summer we can remember, we found ourselves expecting some Very Important People for dinner. When all was ready except a dessert, we had time for an elaborate finale or a run to the beach, but not both. Inspiration, in the form of a well-iced bottle of Sauternes in the back of the refrigerator, led to this creation—quick, easy and elegant. (Our tan looked great at dinner, too!)

1 bottle of good, but not great, French Sauternes, chilled

3 cups fresh raspberries

½ cup Crème Fraîche (recipe follows)

fresh mint leaves (garnish)

RASPBERRY-SAUTERNES DESSERT SOUP

1. Pour the Sauternes into a mixing bowl.

2. Sort through the raspberries, discarding any less-than-perfect berries. Crush about half of the berries with the back of a spoon and stir all of them into the Sauternes. Cover and refrigerate at least 4 hours.

3. Just before serving, measure the *crème fraîche* into a small bowl. Ladle out 2 cups of the chilled Sauternes and whisk it gradually into the *crème fraîche*. Now whisk this mixture back into the remaining Sauternes in the mixing bowl. Ladle into chilled soup bowls or Champagne tulips, apportioning the raspberries fairly, and

garnish each serving with a sprig of fresh mint. Serve immediately.

4 to 6 portions

CRÈME FRAÎCHE

This cultured heavy cream thickens and develops a delicate sour taste as it sits. Spoon it over fruit desserts and fresh berries, with which its tart flavor is delicious. Use it to add body and richness to sauces. Since it can be boiled without fear of separation, it is more versatile than dairy sour cream. Since *crème fraîche* keeps under refrigeration for at least 2 weeks, we are seldom without some in our kitchen.

1 cup heavy cream (not ultra-pasteurized)

1 cup dairy sour cream

1. Whisk heavy cream and sour cream together in a bowl. Cover loosely with plastic wrap and let stand in the kitchen or other reasonably warm spot overnight, or until thickened. In cold weather this may take as long as 24 hours.

2. Cover and refrigerate for at least 4 hours, after which the *crème fraîche* will be quite thick. The tart flavor will continue to develop as the *crème fraîche* sits in the refrigerator.

2 cups

EMON ICE

2 cups strained fresh lemon juice
2 cups water
2 cups granulated sugar

1. Combine lemon juice with water in a small saucepan. Stir in the sugar.

2. Set saucepan over moderate heat. Bring to a boil, stirring constantly, then remove from heat and cool to room temperature.

3. Pour the lemon mixture into a shallow pan (an 8-inch square cake tin is ideal) and set it in your freezer.

4. The ice will be ready in 3 to 6 hours,

depending on the efficiency of your freezer. Because of the high sugar content, this ice will usually be soft enough to serve, so you may as well make it in advance of the day you'll be needing it.

1 quart of very intense ice,
6 or more portions

BLACKBERRY MOUSSE

Search field or market for these black wonders; they're worth it. The flavor and color of the mousse are gorgeous.

- **1 tablespoon unflavored gelatin**

- **2 tablespoons cold water**

- **juice and grated zest of 1 orange**

- **2 pint baskets blackberries, or 2 bags (10 ounces each) frozen berries without sugar; reserve several for garnish**

- **2 egg yolks**

- **½ cup granulated sugar**

2 tablespoons Cointreau

2 cups heavy cream

**2 kiwis, peeled and sliced
(optional garnish)**

1. Soak gelatin in the cold water in a
   saucepan for 5 minutes. Add orange juice,
   grated orange zest and berries, and bring
   just to a boil, stirring. Cool to room
   temperature.

2. Beat egg yolks and sugar in a bowl until
   pale yellow. Add Cointreau and beat for
   another minute.

3. Put egg yolk mixture in the top pan of a
   double boiler over simmering water.

Stir until slightly thickened and hot to the touch. Cool to room temperature.

4. Add egg yolk mixture to blackberry mixture and stir until well blended. Whip heavy cream to soft peaks and fold gently into blackberry and egg yolk mixture. Divide among serving dishes and chill until ready to serve.

5. Garnish with sliced kiwis, each topped with a whole berry, or with berries alone.

8 to 10 portions

MAPLE-HAZELNUT MOUSSE

Delicious and unusual contrast of textures. The silkiness of the mousse and the pleasant crunch of the praline is superb. Serve with pear slices drizzled with a little maple syrup.

Hazelnut Praline (recipe follows)

9 egg yolks, room temperature

3/4 cup pure maple syrup

1½ cups heavy or whipping cream, cold

3 egg whites, room temperature

Pinch cream of tartar

MAPLE-HAZELNUT MOUSSE

1. Make the praline.

2. Beat the egg yolks and syrup in a mixer bowl until the mixture forms a slowly dissolving ribbon when the beaters are lifted. Transfer to the top of a double boiler and whisk over simmering water until the mixture is very thick, about 3 minutes. Remove and let cool completely.

3. Beat the cream until stiff. In a separate bowl with clean beaters, beat the egg whites with the cream of tartar until stiff but not dry. Gently fold the whipped cream into the cooled maple custard; then fold in the egg whites and then the praline.

4. Spoon the mousse into 8 goblets and refrigerate covered several hours.

8 portions

HAZELNUT PRALINE

1½ cups hazelnuts

½ cup sugar

2 tablespoons water

1 teaspoon vanilla extract

1 tablespoon unsalted butter

1. Preheat oven to 350°F.
2. Toast the hazelnuts on a baking sheet for 7 to 10 minutes. Rub the nuts against each other in a kitchen towel to remove the skins.

3. Slowly heat the sugar and water in a heavy medium-size saucepan to boiling. Then boil rapidly for 2 to 3 minutes, stirring occasionally with a wooden spoon. Remove from heat, add the nuts, and stir until evenly coated with syrup. The sugar will start to crystallize.

4. Return to medium heat to melt the sugar again and carmelize the nuts. Cook, stirring constantly with a wooden spoon, until the nuts begin to color. Stir in the vanilla. (If the mixture begins to smoke, remove it immediately from the heat. Allow it to cool slightly before continuing.)

Continue to cook and stir until the nuts turn a nice golden color. Remove from heat and stir in the butter.

5. Spread the praline mixture on an oiled piece of aluminum foil and let stand until completely cooled.

6. Break the cooled praline into pieces and process in a food processor fitted with a steel blade until coarsely chopped. Store the praline in an airtight container.

About 2½ cups

PAVLOVA

Created in honor of the great ballerina.

4 egg whites, at room temperature

¼ teaspoon salt

¼ teaspoon cream of tartar

1 cup fine granulated sugar

4 teaspoons cornstarch

2 teaspoons white wine vinegar

1 teaspoon vanilla extract

1 cup heavy cream, chilled

**2 to 3 cups strawberries,
sliced and sprinkled with
sugar and Grand Marnier**

1. Preheat oven to 275°F.

2. Beat egg whites, salt, and cream of tartar together in a bowl until the whites hold a stiff peak. Add the sugar, a few tablespoons at a time, beating until mixture is stiff and glossy. Beat in the cornstarch, then the vinegar and the vanilla.

3. Butter and lightly flour a loose-bottomed 8-inch cake pan and fill gently with the meringue mixture, spreading it higher around the edges than in the center of the pan to form a depression.

4. Bake cake for 1 to 1¼ hours, or until meringue is firm and lightly browned. Pavlova will remain moist inside. Cool

slightly, unmold, slide onto a serving plate, and cool completely.

5. Lightly whip cream. Just before serving, spread the Pavlova with whipped cream and then with the strawberries. Serve immediately.

4 to 6 portions

OLDE ENGLISH TRIFLE

The traditional British dessert is a festive blend of rich flavors. Layer it decoratively in a favorite glass bowl and sit back and enjoy Christmas—the whole dessert can be prepared ahead of time.

1 Sara Lee pound cake (10¾ ounces), thawed

½ cup seedless raspberry jam

1 cup coarsely broken amaretti

1 cup Marsala

3 tablespoons granulated sugar

1½ tablespoons cornstarch

3 egg yolks

amaretti

2½ cups milk

1 teaspoon vanilla extract

2 cups heavy or whipping cream, cold

3 tablespoons confectioners' sugar

½ teaspoon almond extract

1 cup toasted sliced almonds

Candied red cherries or fresh strawberries (garnish)

1. Cut the cake into ¼-inch slices and spread out flat on a surface to dry for several hours. Spread a thin layer of the jam on half the cake slices. Top with the remaining cake slices. Cut the cake sandwiches into 1-inch

cubes and scatter in a large glass bowl.

2. Add the amaretti crumbs and toss together.
   Sprinkle with Marsala and toss to coat.

3. Whisk the granulated sugar, cornstarch,
   and egg yolks together in a saucepan.
   Whisk in the milk in a thin, steady stream.
   Cook, stirring constantly, over medium
   heat until thickened to the consistency of a
   custard. Remove from heat and whisk in
   the vanilla. Let cool completely.

4. Pour the cooled custard over the
   cake mixture.

5. Whip the cream in a chilled bowl until soft
   peaks form. Beat in the confectioners'
   sugar and almond extract and continue

beating until stiff. Pipe the flavored cream over the top of the trifle using a pastry bag, or spoon it over decoratively. Scatter the almonds over the top. Refrigerate, covered with plastic wrap, until ready to serve, up to 3 days.

6. Spoon the trifle into glass bowls and garnish with candied cherries.

8 to 10 portions

CARROT CAKE

In the beginning, Sheila's mother drove her famous carrot cakes down to Manhattan daily from her Connecticut kitchen. The cake became a Silver Palate classic; it may now become yours as well.

3 cups unbleached all-purpose flour

3 cups granulated sugar

1 teaspoon salt

1 tablespoon baking soda

1 tablespoon ground cinnamon

1½ cups corn oil

4 large eggs, lightly beaten

CARROT CAKE

1 tablespoon vanilla extract

1½ cups shelled walnuts, chopped

1½ cups shredded coconut

1⅓ cups puréed cooked carrots

¾ cup drained crushed pineapple

Cream-Cheese Frosting
(recipe follows)

confectioners' sugar for dusting top

1. Preheat oven to 350°F. Grease two 9-inch
   springform pans.

2. Sift dry ingredients into a bowl. Add oil,
   eggs and vanilla. Beat well. Fold in
   walnuts, coconut, carrots, and pineapple.

3. Pour batter into the prepared pans. Set on

the middle rack of the oven and bake for 50 minutes, until edges have pulled away from sides and a cake tester inserted in center comes out clean.

4. Cool on a cake rack for 3 hours. Fill cake and frost sides with cream-cheese frosting. Dust top with confectioners' sugar.

10 to 12 portions

CREAM-CHEESE FROSTING

**8 ounces cream cheese,
   at room temperature**

**6 tablespoons sweet butter,
   at room temperature**

3 cups confectioners' sugar

1 teaspoon vanilla extract

juice of ½ lemon (optional)

1. Cream together cream cheese and butter in
   a mixing bowl.

2. Slowly sift in confectioners' sugar and
   continue beating until fully incorporated.
   Mixture should be free of lumps.

3. Stir in vanilla, and lemon juice if you
   use it.

Frosting for a 2-layer cake

B ANANA CAKE

Lush and delicious.

- ½ pound (2 sticks) sweet butter
- 1 cup granulated sugar
- 2 eggs
- 1 cup mashed ripe bananas
- 1¾ cups unbleached all-purpose flour
- ½ teaspoon salt
- ⅔ teaspoon baking soda
- 5 tablespoons buttermilk
- 1 teaspoon vanilla extract

BANANA CAKE

**Cream-Cheese Frosting
(see page 100)**

**1½ to 2 medium-size, firm but
ripe, bananas, sliced**

1½ cups shelled, chopped walnuts

1. Preheat oven to 350°F. Grease and flour two 9-inch layer cake pans.

2. Cream butter and sugar together until light and fluffy. Add eggs, one at a time, beating well after each addition. Add mashed bananas, mixing thoroughly.

3. Sift dry ingredients and add to butter and egg mixture. Stir until flour has been incorporated completely. Add buttermilk and vanilla. Mix for 1 minute.

4. Pour batter into the prepared pans. Set on the middle rack of the oven and bake for 25 to 30 minutes or until a cake tester inserted into the center comes out clean.

5. Cool in pans on a rack for 10 minutes. Unmold and cool on rack for 2 hours.

6. When cooled, place one layer on a serving plate and frost with Cream-Cheese Frosting. Arrange slices of banana over frosting; cover with second layer and frost top and sides of cake.

7. Cover sides of cake with chopped nuts,

holding in palm and pressing firmly to sides of cake. Dust top of cake with confectioners' sugar.

10 to 12 portions

ORANGE POPPY-SEED BUNDT CAKE

8 tablespoons (1 stick) sweet butter, at room temperature

1½ cups granulated sugar

4 eggs

2 cups unbleached all-purpose flour

2½ teaspoons baking powder

½ teaspoon salt

¾ cup milk

½ cup poppy seeds

1 teaspoon vanilla extract

grated zest of 2 oranges

double recipe Orange Glaze (recipe follows)

ORANGE POPPY-SEED BUNDT CAKE

1. Preheat oven to 325°F. Grease a 10-inch bundt pan.

2. Cream butter and sugar together in a mixing bowl until light and fluffy. Add eggs, one at a time, beating well after each addition.

3. Sift flour, baking powder, and salt together. Add to creamed mixture alternately with milk. Mix well after each addition.

4. Fold in poppy seeds, vanilla, and grated orange zest. Pour batter into the prepared bundt pan.

5. Set on the middle rack of the oven and bake for 50 to 60 minutes, or until edges

shrink away slightly from sides of pan and a cake tester inserted into the center comes out clean. Let cake cool in the pan for 30 minutes before turning it out onto a cake rack.

6. When cake has cooled, prick holes in it 1½ inches apart with a long toothpick, and pour the Orange Glaze evenly over top. Serve warm with ice cream on side.

12 portions

ORANGE GLAZE

¼ cup fresh orange juice
¼ cup granulated sugar

Combine orange juice and sugar in a small saucepan and simmer gently for 5 minutes, stirring occasionally, until a light syrup forms.

C HESTNUT CAKE

Light and moist, our favorite yellow cake.

2 cups granulated sugar

4 eggs

1 cup vegetable oil

1 cup dry white wine

2½ cups unbleached all-purpose flour

½ teaspoon salt

2¼ teaspoons baking powder

1 teaspoon vanilla extract

Chocolate Icing (see page 123), warm

¾ cup sweetened chestnut puree*

whole chestnuts preserved in syrup* (optional garnish)

1. Preheat oven to 350°F. Grease and flour two 9-inch round layer cake pans.

2. Beat sugar and eggs together, using an electric mixer, for 30 seconds on medium speed. Add oil, wine, flour, salt, baking powder and vanilla; beat for 1 minute.

3. Pour batter into the prepared pans. Set on the middle rack of the oven and bake for 30 minutes, or until cake has pulled away from sides of pan and a knife inserted in the center comes out clean.

4. Let cakes cool in pans for 5 minutes. Turn them out on rack and let cool for at least 2 hours before frosting.

5. Arrange 1 cake layer on a serving plate. Spread with warm chocolate icing. Set second layer on top of first and spread with chestnut purée. Cover sides of cake with remaining icing. Decorate top with well-drained whole preserved chestnuts if desired. Chill cake for 45 minutes before serving.

8 or more portions

*available at specialty food shops

BITTERSWEET CHOCOLATE CAKE

- **14 ounces semisweet chocolate (the darkest you can find)**

- **3 tablespoons cold water**

- **12 eggs, separated**

- **2 cups granulated sugar**

- **¾ pound plus 4 tablespoons (3½ sticks) sweet butter, softened**

- **1 cup unbleached all-purpose flour, sifted**

- **confectioners' sugar**

1. Preheat oven to 325°F. Butter and sugar a 10-inch spring-form pan and tap out any extra sugar.

2. Grate or break chocolate into small pieces. Place in top part of a double boiler with the cold water. Melt over simmering water, whisking until smooth. Let chocolate cool slightly.

3. Beat egg yolks with the granulated sugar until they are thick and pale yellow and form a ribbon when they fall from the beater. Fold in warm chocolate. Stir in the very soft butter and then fold in the sifted flour. Mix thoroughly but gently.

4. Beat egg whites until stiff. Stir a large spoonful of the chocolate mixture into the beaten egg whites. Mix well. Pour this mixture into chocolate mixture; fold

together gently, incorporating whites completely. Be very careful at this stage not to overmix.

5. Turn batter into the springform pan. It will come close to the top of the pan. Set on the middle rack of the oven and bake for 1 hour and 20 minutes, or until cake tester inserted in center comes out clean. Cool on rack for 15 minutes, then remove outer rim. Allow cake to cool completely before removing bottom of pan. Refrigerate.

6. When ready to serve, using a paper doily as a stencil, sprinkle with confectioners' sugar to make a design. Serve cold.

20 small but sweet portions

C HOCOLATE HAZELNUT CAKE

The best chocolate cake in the universe.

4 eggs, separated

1 cup granulated sugar

4 ounces unsweetened chocolate

12 tablespoons (1½ sticks) sweet butter

1 cup plus 1 tablespoon cake flour

¼ teaspoon salt

3 tablespoons very finely ground skinned hazelnuts

Hazelnut Buttercream (recipe follows)

Chocolate Icing (recipe follows)

8 whole hazelnuts (garnish)

CHOCOLATE HAZELNUT CAKE

1. Beat egg yolks and sugar together until mixture is thick and pale yellow.

2. Meanwhile, in the top part of a double boiler set over simmering water, melt the chocolate with the butter, whisking constantly until smooth; cool slightly.

3. Preheat oven to 350°F. Grease an 8-inch springform pan. Line the bottom with a circle of wax paper. Grease the paper and lightly flour lining and sides of pan.

4. Pour chocolate-butter mixture into egg mixture and stir just to blend. Fold in flour, salt and ground hazelnuts.

5. Whip egg whites until stiff and fold gently into batter.

6. Pour the cake batter into prepared pan and rap the pan lightly on a work surface to eliminate any air bubbles.

7. Set on the middle rack of the oven and bake for 35 to 40 minutes, or until edges are firm and inside is set but still somewhat soft. Do not worry if top cracks slightly. Cool in the pan, set on a rack, for 1 hour. Remove sides of pan and cool cake to room temperature.

8. When cake is cool, invert it onto a serving plate and spread top and

sides with hazelnut buttercream. Refrigerate cake for 30 minutes.

9. Remove cake from refrigerator and spread top and sides with warm chocolate icing. Work quickly, as icing sets.

10. Decorate the top of the cake with 8 whole hazelnuts. Refrigerate the cake for at least 1 hour before cutting and serving.

1 cake, 8 portions

HAZELNUT BUTTERCREAM

1¼ cups shelled hazelnuts

5 tablespoons corn syrup

2 tablespoons brandy

1 cup confectioners' sugar, sifted

4 tablespoons sweet butter, softened

1. Roast hazelnuts on a baking sheet in a 350°F oven for 10 to 15 minutes, or until their skins have loosened. Remove from oven and rub between towels to remove skins.

2. Transfer to the bowl of a food processor fitted with a steel blade, and run machine until nuts begin to form a paste, like peanut butter in texture.

HAZELNUT BUTTERCREAM

3. Scrape paste into a bowl and stir in corn syrup and brandy. Let sit for 20 minutes. (Can be prepared in advance and refrigerated. Let return to room temperature before proceeding with recipe.)

4. Cream confectioners' sugar and butter together until light and fluffy. Add hazelnut paste and mix thoroughly.

Enough for top and sides of one 8-inch layer

CHOCOLATE ICING

4 tablespoons sweet butter

4 ounces semisweet chocolate

3 tablespoons cream

2/3 cup sifted confectioners' sugar, approximately

1 teaspoon vanilla extract

1. Melt butter and chocolate together in the top part of a double boiler over simmering water, whisking constantly.

2. Remove pan from heat and beat in cream. Sift in confectioners' sugar and vanilla. Icing should be very smooth. Spread while warm.

Enough for top and sides of one 8-inch cake layer

DECADENT CHOCOLATE CAKE

The name says it all.

1 cup boiling water

3 ounces unsweetened chocolate

8 tablespoons (1 stick) sweet butter

1 teaspoon vanilla extract

2 cups granulated sugar

2 eggs, separated

1 teaspoon baking soda

½ cup dairy sour cream

2 cups less 2 tablespoons unbleached,
  all-purpose flour, sifted

1 teaspoon baking powder

Chocolate Frosting (recipe follows)

1. Preheat oven to 350°F. Grease and flour a 10-inch tube pan. Knock out excess.

2. Pour boiling water over chocolate and butter; let stand until melted. Stir in vanilla and sugar, then whisk in egg yolks, one at a time, blending well after each addition.

3. Mix baking soda and sour cream and whisk into chocolate mixture.

4. Sift flour and baking powder together and add to batter, mixing thoroughly.

5. Beat egg whites until stiff but not dry. Stir a quarter of the egg whites

thoroughly into the batter. Scoop remaining egg whites on top of the batter and gently fold together.

6. Pour batter into the prepared pan. Set on the middle rack of the oven and bake for 40 to 50 minutes, or until the edges have pulled away from the sides of the pan and a cake tester inserted into the center comes out clean. Cool in pan for 10 minutes; unmold and cool completely before frosting.

12 portions